THE ULTIMATE GUIDE TO A

GREAT SEX

50 sealed, sexual games for lovers...
each one guaranteed to tease and tantalize
the hungriest sexual appetites.

Tear out the pages to reveal one hot, sensuous
adventure after another!!!

A must for every lover everywhere!!!

Compiled from
stories and suggestions
contributed by lovers nationwide

Edited By:
Alex and Elizabeth Lluch

Published by Wedding Solutions Publishing, Inc

© Copyright 2002

All rights reserved under International and Pan-American Copyright Conventions. No part of this book may be reproduced or transmitted in any form or by any means, electronic or mechanical, including photocopy, recording or by any information storage and retrieval system, without permission in writing from the publisher.

Printed in China

ISBN 1-887169-28-8

INTRODUCTION

The Ultimate Guide To Great Sex is the second in a series of books written for men and women who are wanting to add some spice to their sexual lives. Whether you are young and a bit inexperienced, older and caught in a routine, in a new relationship or have been together for years, *The Ultimate Guide To Great Sex* is for you.

Are you ready to make your sex life sizzle? This book contains 50 sealed pages – 25 for the woman to pleasure her lover and 25 for the man to pleasure his lover. It is indicated at the bottom of each page whether the game is to be selected by the man or the woman. Let the titles titillate your senses and your imagination and then tear open the sealed page to reveal the day's (or night's) romantically seductive events. Take turns choosing one of these special adventures and get ready to enjoy new ways of kindling or rekindling the flames of desire for one another.

The Ultimate Guide To Great Sex contains a wide variety of experiences to share with your mate. Use these encounters to add some extra lust to your love life. Some of the games may make you feel as if you are taking a "walk on the wild side." It's natural to have some hesitations about trying something daring and new, but that is exactly why you are holding this book! Test your sense of adventure. Have some fun exploring different ways of arousing and satisfying one another. Get wet and wild, frisky and free! Most of all, have fun!

Your reward for reading *The Ultimate Guide To Great Sex?* Spicy, steamy, sizzling sex and a new found passion for that special someone in your life! What are you waiting for?

TABLE OF CONTENTS

GREAT
SEX GAME
#1

DANCE OF THE
SEVEN VEILS

For the
Woman

Turn him into
your Arabian Night!

to pleasure
her lover

Nicknames for Her

Mount of Venus

Nectar Unit

Candy Box

Pot O' Gold

Big Boy's Joy

GREAT
SEX GAME
#2

VIVA LAS VEGAS

For the
Man

Take a trip
to the Strip!

to pleasure
his lover

Nicknames for Him

Purple Helmet
Soldier of Love
Hard Drive
Mr. Happy
Tube Steak

GREAT
SEX GAME
#3

TURN UP THE HEAT

For the
Woman

Alert the Fire Department

before you begin!

to pleasure
her lover

Kissing Turn-Ons

Both men and women equally are turned on by
French kissing, as well as kissing in public.

Women, however, enjoy a little
playful biting more so than their mates.

Ear nibbling? Twice as many women
as men find it makes them hot.

But the biggest difference
is their response to neck kissing:
women outnumber men 10 to 1 favoring
neck licks as their prelude to passion.

GREAT SEX GAME #4

VARIETY IS THE SPICE OF LIFE

For the
Man

A hot night may
be in the cards tonight!

to pleasure
his lover

Bring Back the Romance

Cover your bed with rose petals

Send a singing telegram

Give love coupons

Watch the sunrise or sunset, with
champagne and strawberries

Leave the dishes 'til tomorrow

GREAT
SEX GAME
#5

COFFEE, TEA, OR ME?

For the
Woman

Breakfast

of Champions!

to pleasure
her lover

Gadgets for the Adventurous Female
(For him to use on her!)

Nipple Clamps
Ben Wa Balls
Clit Clips
Remote Control Vibrator
Riding Crop

GREAT
SEX GAME
#6

WAIT AND SEE

For the
Man

A gift a day keeps

the boredom away!

to pleasure
his lover

Gadgets for the Adventurous Male
(For her to use on him!)

Cock Ring
Penis Pump
Harness
Anal Plug
Edible Gel

GREAT
SEX GAME
#7

PICTURE THIS!

For the
Woman

Has he been working late?

Not tonight!

to pleasure
her lover

Herbal Aphrodisiacs
(Consult your doctor first!)

Damiana – a sexual stimulant
Saw Palmetto – increases libido
Ginseng – increases stamina
Chinese Angelica – an overall sexual stimulant

GREAT
SEX GAME
#8

KIDNAP!

For the
Man

She'll be bound
to pay this ransom!

to pleasure
his lover

Masturbation Nicknames

Spank the Monkey
Polish the Pearl
Make a Milkshake
Unbutton the Fur Coat
Playing Pocket Pool
Petting the Bunny
Fingerpainting
Sex With Someone You Love
Choke the Chicken
Roughing Up the Suspect

GREAT
SEX GAME
#9

THE CHEERLEADER

For the
Woman

Score the

winning goal!

to pleasure
her lover

Put My Lips Where?

Don't always go for the obvious!
Have you tried...
the underarm?
the perineum?
the navel?
between the toes?
the small of the back?
the back of the knees?
the bottom of the feet?
the big toe?

GREAT
SEX GAME
#10

KINKY KALLING KARD

For the
Man

Dial "S"
for Sex!

to pleasure
his lover

Stock Your Library

The Kama Sutra
Nudes
The Erotic Lives of Women
The Claiming of Sleeping Beauty
Secret Sexual Positions
Erotic Massage: The Touch of Love
Passion Play
The Ultimate Kiss
Awakening the Virgin
The Mammoth Book of Erotica
The Joy of Sex
The Sensuous Woman

GREAT
SEX GAME
#11

HOME MOVIES

For the
Woman

Direct and
produce his pleasure!

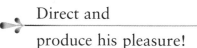

to pleasure
her lover

A Simple Secret

Locking eyes with a lover is
the most intimate act you can
perform when making love.

GREAT
SEX GAME
#12

MAGIC FINGERS

For the
Man

Give me your tired, your
poor, your oiled muscles...

to pleasure
his lover

How Does Passion Rate?

78% of men and 74% of women surveyed
name passion as the #1 essential element
for a healthy, long-term relationship.

Think you've lost it? There's hope!
Most people are optimistic –
68% of men and 86% of women are confident
they can recapture it! They're probably holding
this book in their hands right now!

GREAT
SEX GAME
#13

MAGNIFICENT MISTRESS

For the
Woman

You'll have him

eating out of your...hand!

to pleasure
her lover

Did You Know?

Women <u>do</u> ejaculate!
A woman's "love juice" is usually
anywhere from ½ to 1 teaspoon of
a milky, non-staining substance.

GREAT SEX GAME #14

HAREM NIGHTS

For the
Man

Create an
oasis in your home!

to pleasure
his lover

Keeping It Up

Young men "raise the flag" automatically.
With time and the security of a long-term
relationship, men need three things to
become sexually aroused:

Intimacy

Pleasure

Eroticism

GREAT
SEX GAME
#15

FUN WITH FIGURES

For the
Woman

Your mission, should
you decide to accept it...

to pleasure
her lover

Looking for Her Secret Spots?

Her secret spot is NOT the G-spot!
Men, don't worry about having to identify
any one given area! Concentrate, instead,
on <u>any</u> one body part – her shoulder,
her foot, her temples – and spend time
massaging just that area. Your patience
and willingness to spend uninterrupted time
just for her will have her wet, craving,
and practically weeping for your
penetrating conclusion!

GREAT SEX GAME #16

MY TUTOR

For the
Man

You'll be the
teacher's pet!

to pleasure
his lover

Looking for His Secret Spots?

Try these:

Buttocks
Balls
Ears
Nipples
Perineum
Inner Thigh
Anus

GREAT
SEX GAME
#17

LADY OF THE NIGHT

For the
Woman

She's not selling
girl scout cookies!

to pleasure
her lover

Excuses Women Use
Why Not To Have Sex

"I have a headache..."
"My hair is dirty..."
"The draperies aren't hanging right..."
"My mother might call..."
"Dinner will burn..."
"The neighbors will hear..."
"My legs are hairy..."
"The batteries in the vibrator are dead..."
"You've had a long day..."
"My leather corset is at the dry cleaners..."

GREAT
SEX GAME
#18

SUPER CYBERSEX

For the
Man

Take your
lust online!

to pleasure
his lover

Excuses Men Use
Why Not to Have Sex

GREAT
SEX GAME
#19

AFTERNOON DELIGHT

For the
Woman

As the sun is setting,
he will be rising...

to pleasure
her lover

Imagination!

A little experimentation, combined with imagination, results in getting rid of the boredom of your normal routines! What could YOU do with some of the everyday items you have around the house?

A roll of electrical tape

A hairbrush

A lambswool duster

A bottle of olive oil

A frond from your fern plant

A cotton swab

GREAT
SEX GAME
#20

HER BEST FRIEND

For the
Man

And you thought
three was a crowd!

to pleasure
his lover

Attitude is Everything

The sexiest women are <u>not</u> the ones with
the perkiest tits, the taut butt, the tiny
waist, or the long, slender legs.
The sexiest women are the ones
who <u>think</u> they are sexy!

GREAT
SEX GAME
#21

VIVA LA DIFFERENCE!

For the
Woman

Maid
to please!

to pleasure
her lover

Acting Out Fantasies
(For Him)

Cowboy

Priest

Gigolo

Delivery Boy

Movie Director

Slave

Gynecologist

Police Man

Construction Worker

GREAT SEX GAME #22

THE SEXUAL TRIVIA TEST

For the
Man

Excuse me,
do I know you?

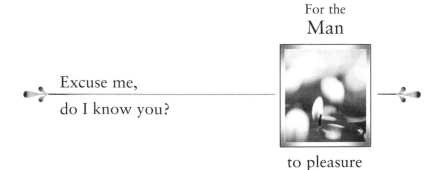

to pleasure
his lover

Acting Out Fantasies
(For Her)

Virgin

Librarian

Cheerleader

Stewardess

Prostitute

Farmer's Daughter

Sex Therapist

Teacher

GREAT
SEX GAME
#23

SPIN THE BOTTLE

For the
Woman

A very "adult" version
of a children's game!

to pleasure
her lover

What Women Want

The most desired activity a woman wants
from the man she is involved with is for
him to cook her dinner.

Women identify preparing a meal
with signs of nurturing,
feeding the soul as well as the body.

GREAT
SEX GAME
#24

IN THE MOOD

For the
Man

You'll have her
where you want her!

to pleasure
his lover

Pet Peeve

Ladies, does it hurt your feelings that your
man is sound asleep almost immediately after
making love with you? Know this: even without
the physical exertion and release that comes
from sex, the average person falls asleep in
just seven minutes! So as he is drifting off
to sweet dreams, know that your love-
making simply accelerated the process.

Great
Sex Game
#25

DINNER AT THE RITZ

For the
Woman

Guess who's coming

AT dinner!

to pleasure
her lover

Fight or Flight

When confronted with conflict, there is a
basic, animal instinct known as the
"Fight or Flight Syndrome."
We either gear up for battle or run away.
Choose your battles carefully and
consider an alternative –
FLOW!

GREAT
SEX GAME
#26

CAMPING UNDER
THE SHEETS

For the
Man

You'll earn your

merit badge tonight!

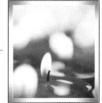

to pleasure
his lover

Five Vital Elements for a Happy Marriage

Make Love
Listen
Make Love
Apologize
Make Love
Forgive
Make Love
Support
Make Love
Touch

Did we mention MAKE LOVE?

GREAT
SEX GAME
#27

SWING HIGH, SWING LOW,
SWING DEEP

For the
Woman

Playground

pleasures!

to pleasure
her lover

Understanding Women

To love a woman is to understand her
...or at least pretend to.

For women, love is an occupation
...smart men take on love as a second job.

Married women start appearing with
green goop on their faces in the name of beauty.

Women are more creative than men
...they need to tell men how great they are.

Diamonds are a girl's best friend and
dogs are a man's – now who's smarter?

GREAT
SEX GAME
#28

MARDI GRAS

For the
Man

Man's search
for sexual pleasure!

to pleasure
his lover

Understanding Men

A woman marries a man,
expecting she can change him...she can't.

Men wake up in the morning as good-looking
as they were when they went to sleep.

Men think, dream, and talk about sex
more than any other topic.

All men are good for the first year...
then the warranty runs out.

Men's faults: everything they say and
everything they do.

GREAT
SEX GAME
#29

TAKE IT OFF...
TAKE IT ALL OFF

It's not
Avon calling!

For the
Woman

to pleasure
her lover

To Be United

See with your Mind
Touch with your Heart
Laugh with your Soul
Listen with Love

GREAT
SEX GAME
#30

THE HONEY POT

For the
Man

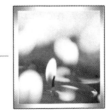

You won't want to get
out of this sticky situation!

to pleasure
his lover

Forget the Gym!

Ladies, do you spend time at the gym,
lifting weights, doing aerobics, cycling for
hours to firm and tighten every muscle you
have, and some you didn't know you have?
NEVER forget the most important
muscle you possess!
Do your kegel exercises daily – in the car,
standing in line, sitting in a business meeting and,
most importantly, while you have his
hot cock inside you! Squeeze, then release;
squeeze, then release; squeeze, then release!
You'll intensify his pleasure and your own.
He'll worship the ground you walk on
and overlook what gravity does
to the rest of your body!

GREAT SEX GAME #31

THE BIGGEST VIBRATOR EVER MADE

For the
Woman

Take your
love life for a spin!

to pleasure
her lover

What Women Need for Great Sex

1. Reciprocal love
2. Commitment
3. Feeling safe, physically and emotionally
4. Mutual acceptance

GREAT
SEX GAME
#32

SEX EDUCATION

For the
Man

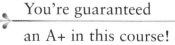

You're guaranteed
an A+ in this course!

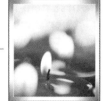

to pleasure
his lover

Build a Time Capsule

Capture your love, your memories,
your treasures, your secrets, and your past
to put away for your future.

Build a time capsule together!
Collect old love notes, favorite sayings,
a flower from your wedding, your first love song,
a sentimental photo – anything that has special
meaning for the two of you. Tuck your collection on
a shelf to bring out, review, add to and store away as
a testament to your love and your lives together.

GREAT SEX GAME #33

PHONE HOME

For the
Woman

ET would never
have been left behind!

to pleasure
her lover

Know and Respect the Differences

Men are very turned on by visual stimuli –
just look at the number and variety of men's
magazines of erotic images. Men like the lights on
when they make love. They want to see the
reactions and the results of their prowess!

Women want to hide! They fear performance
pressure. They want lights out!

So take turns! Loving is all about giving what your
partner wants, instead of only what you want.

GREAT
SEX GAME
#34

For the
Man

A night of
"fine" art!

to pleasure
his lover

As Women Age

When asked if they had achieved sexual ecstasy,
85% of women aged 20 – 30 said yes.
That increased to 89% for women 30 – 40
and 91% for women over 40.
Correspondingly, anxiety over her body
image decreased with age.
63% of women 20 – 30 and 30 – 40
report that concerns with their body image and
performance gets in the way of satisfying sex.
That percentage decreases with age!
51% for women 40 – 50 and
46% for women over 50.

GREAT
SEX GAME
#35

KISSES FROM THE HEART

For the
Woman

Sugar and spice
and everything nice!

to pleasure
her lover

Should We Or Shouldn't We?

46% of men surveyed and 34% of women say
that some form of soft pornography is a
regular prelude to their passion play.

GREAT
SEX GAME
#36

LOVE IN THE BACKSEAT

For the
Man

Go back
to the future!

to pleasure
his lover

Do Something Different!

Breaking your routine is what it's all about!

Buy a Wonderbra
Try a temporary body tattoo
Switch to a garter belt and hose
Order body jewelry (waist chains are sexy)
Out with the flannel, in with silk and satin

GREAT SEX GAME #37

LAP DANCE...
THE LAST DANCE OF LOVE

For the
Woman

Sway to the beat...
of his racing heart!

to pleasure
her lover

Nicknames for Breasts

The Pointer Sisters
Pom-Poms
Golden Nuggets
Mounds of Joy
Pleasure Pebbles

GREAT
SEX GAME
#38

THE FORBIDDEN ZONE

For the
Man

You'll be "stalling"
for pleasure!

to pleasure
his lover

Take It or Leave It
But You Can't Change It!

Single men are reported to have
solo sex (masturbate) one to two times a day.

Married men still masturbate!
Reportedly only one to two times a week, but
nonetheless they still engage in
self-pleasuring themselves.

What women need to know is that this is no
reflection on their man's satisfaction with
their sex life with their life partner.
In fact, most say they are thinking of
their beloved, not some fictional creature!
So accept it, even offer to help, but
don't take it personally!

GREAT
SEX GAME
#39

THE HONEY-DO LIST

For the
Woman

Let the "Master Craftsman" strut his stuff!

to pleasure
her lover

An Erotic Meal

Part of what makes a food an
aphrodisiac is its erotic shape.

Plan a dinner that will plant
food for thought!

Consider using:
Avocados
Fresh Figs
Chiles
Black Beans
Bananas
Oysters in the Shell
Onion Rings
Ice Cream Cone
Cucumbers

GREAT
SEX GAME
#40

THE EXERCISE INSTRUCTOR

For the
Man

Keeping fit

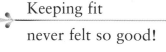

never felt so good!

to pleasure
his lover

What Would You Do If You Had a Penis For A Day?

Some of the women surveyed answered:

"I would measure it both ways."

"I would play with it all day."

"I would see how many donuts I could carry with it."

"I would want a big one and then I would show it to everyone."

"I would jump up and down and watch it swing all around."

And what would your pleasure be?

GREAT
SEX GAME
#41

LET'S EAT

For the
Woman

Who says you can't
have dessert before dinner?

to pleasure
her lover

Theory of "Connectivity"

Women need to make a connection
before they make love.

Men need to make love
in order to feel a connection.

GREAT
SEX GAME
#42

RENT-A-ROOM

For the
Man

You won't be able to wipe
that blush off your face!

to pleasure
his lover

Increase Your Satisfaction!

77% of women polled who rate their
sexual satisfaction as "Very High" also admit
they read both romantic and erotic
literature on a regular basis.

GREAT
SEX GAME
#43

TOGAS AND TUBS

For the
Woman

Oh mighty Ceaser,
how can I serve thee?

to pleasure
her lover

Dance The Night Away

The reason dancing is considered an
act of foreplay is that it is a vertical
act of a horizontal desire.

GREAT
SEX GAME
#44

THE GIFT OF TIME

For the
Man

Special moments
for your lady love!

to pleasure
his lover

Nicknames for "The Act"

Carnal Communication

Hole-In-One

Rub the Lamp and Let the Genie Out

Slam Dunk

Kinky Kontact

Makin' Whoopee

Horizontal Tango

GREAT
SEX GAME
#45

SPREAD 'EM

For the
Woman

You'll need to
frisk this desperado!

to pleasure
her lover

The Love Indicator

Clasp your hands together, lacing your fingers.
Look to see which thumb is on top!
If your right thumb is on top, pointing
toward your heart...you're a lover!
If your left thumb is on top...
you wish you were!

GREAT
SEX GAME
#46

HER PLEASURE PALACE

For the
Man

Need to get back
into her good graces?

to pleasure
his lover

Gifts For The Senses

An Aromatherapy Machine – a heat-activated device
that you fill with aromatic beads, such as
"Rejuvenation," "Relaxation," or "Invigoration."
Fill your room with delightful scents.

A Body Massaging Mat – whether one for
the full body or just back and seat, these
stimulating mats send different rates
and intensities of pulsing massage.

Sound Machine – choose from a variety of
peaceful sounds, including rhythmic ocean waves,
a babbling brook, a gentle spring rain, or the
sultry sounds of a summer night.

GREAT
SEX GAME
#47

PICTURE PERFECT

For the
Woman

A photo album

you won't want to share!

to pleasure
her lover

Bored?
Try These Board Games

Romantic Rendezvous
Talk Dirty to Me
Hearts are Wild
Between the Sheets
Sexual Secrets
An Enchanting Evening
The Game of Hot Seat
The Erogenous Zone Game
Intimate Commands
Strip Bingo
More Foreplay, The Game
Sensuous Exciting Experiences
Getting to Know You...Better
SeXplay

These games can be purchased at most
adult sex shops or catalogs.

GREAT
SEX GAME
#48

YOU'VE BEEN SO NAUGHTY

For the
Man

Teach her an
unforgettable lesson!

to pleasure
his lover

Wet and Wild Ways
To Be Playful

Wet T-shirt contests in your shower

In a public pool

Dashing through a backyard sprinkler

In the backseat of your car during a rain storm

Catch those jets in your Jacuzzi

Wash the car and hose each other down

Luxurious bubble baths

GREAT
SEX GAME
#49

THE OFFICE VISIT

For the
Woman

Show him
who's boss!

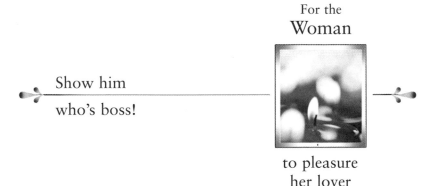

to pleasure
her lover

Say It Again, Sam

English.......	I Love You
French........	Je T'aime
German......	Ich Liebe Dich
Spanish.......	Te Amo
Italian.........	Ti Amo
Japanese......	Ai Shite Imasu
Chinese.......	Wo Ai Ni
Hawaiian.....	Aloha Wau Ia Oe
Russian........	Ya Lyublyu Tyebya
Greek..........	S'Agapo

GREAT SEX GAME #50

I'VE BEEN WATCHING YOU

For the
Man

You'll be her

"Stranger in the Night"!

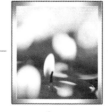

to pleasure
his lover

Aroma Therapy
Creating Your Mood With Scents

For over 6,000 years, fragrances extracted from
flowers, herbs, and spices have been used
to stimulate different moods. Experiment
with just one scent, or a combination.

Sensual	~	Rose Absolute
Enticing	~	Ylang-Ylang
Invigorating	~	Pine
Euphoric	~	Clary Sage
Clearing	~	Eucalyptus
Spicy	~	Ginger
Aphrodisiac	~	Jasmine
Refreshing	~	Lemon
Radiance	~	Orange
Balancing	~	Geranium
Rejuvenating	~	Linden Blossom
Relaxing	~	Mandarin
Serenity	~	Palmarosa
Stimulant	~	Rosemary